MARIE CURIE

DISCOVER THE LIFE OF AN INVENTOR

Don McLeese

Rourke Publishing LLC
Vero Beach, Florida 32964

www.rourkepublishing.com

PHOTO CREDITS: Cover ©Time Life Pictures/Getty Pictures; Title, pgs 15, 16, 18 ©AIP/Emilio Segre Visual Archives; pgs 4, 8, 10, 21 from the Library of Congress; pg 13 ©Getty Images; pg 7, courtesy of the University of Pennsylvania Library

Title page: *A photograph of Marie and Pierre Curie taken in 1904.*

Library of Congress Cataloging-in-Publication Data

McLeese, Don.
  Marie Curie / Don McLeese.
     p. cm. -- (Discover the life of an inventor II)
  Includes bibliographical references and index.
  ISBN 1-59515-431-0
  1. Curie, Marie, 1867-1934--Juvenile literature. 2.
Chemists--Poland--Biography--Juvenile literature. I. Title.
  QD22.C8B57 2006
  540'.92--dc22

                          2005011431
Printed in the USA

                    Rourke Publishing
                    1-800-394-7055
                  www.rourkepublishing.com
                  sales@rourkepublishing.com
        Post Office Box 3328, Vero Beach, FL 32964

TABLE OF CONTENTS

TWO NOBEL PRIZES

In the early years of the 1900s, Marie Curie established herself as one of the most important **scientists** in the world. The Nobel Prize is the highest award a scientist can win. Marie won two of them! And she did so at a time when many colleges didn't even allow women to study science.

Marie Curie in an undated photo

With her husband Pierre, Marie discovered a new **element** called **radium**. Doctors were able to use radium to help discover what was wrong with some sick patients and to help them get better. Marie Curie's work with radium changed modern medicine and continues to help save people's lives.

In this illustration of the Curies, Pierre is holding their discovery, radium.

A POLISH GIRL CALLED MANYA

Marie was born on November 7, 1867, in Warsaw. This is the largest city in the country of Poland. Her parents named her Maria Sklodowska. Everyone called her by her nickname, Manya.

Both of her parents were teachers, and they told their daughter how important it was to study hard at school. Manya was one of the smartest students in school. She finished high school when she was only 15!

A WOMAN STUDYING SCIENCE!

Back then, women almost never became scientists. In fact, women weren't even allowed to enter the university in Warsaw. Manya went to work taking care of children and teaching them. She hoped to save up enough money to go to college in Paris, France. When she was 24 she had enough money to go there.

BECOMING MARIE

In Paris, she went to a very famous university called the Sorbonne. She also changed her name to "Marie," which was more common in France than Maria. She studied a lot of science and math. She earned a **scholarship** in **physics** because she was such a good student.

Marie Curie at age 24, shortly after she arrived in Paris

FINDING A LAB. . . AND A HUSBAND!

Marie needed a **laboratory** where she could do **experiments**. A scientist named Pierre Curie said she could use his lab. The two of them fell in love and married.

Marie had planned to return to Warsaw after college, but she stayed in Paris after marrying Pierre. Her name was now Marie Curie.

The Curies in Paris around 1902

IMPORTANT DISCOVERIES

In 1895, the year that Marie and Pierre married, other scientists began experimenting with rays. One ray was the X ray, which could travel through wood or even a person's skin. Another was the ray given off by **uranium**. Marie decided to experiment with the uranium ray. She discovered that there was another element within uranium that was producing the rays.

Marie Curie in her laboratory

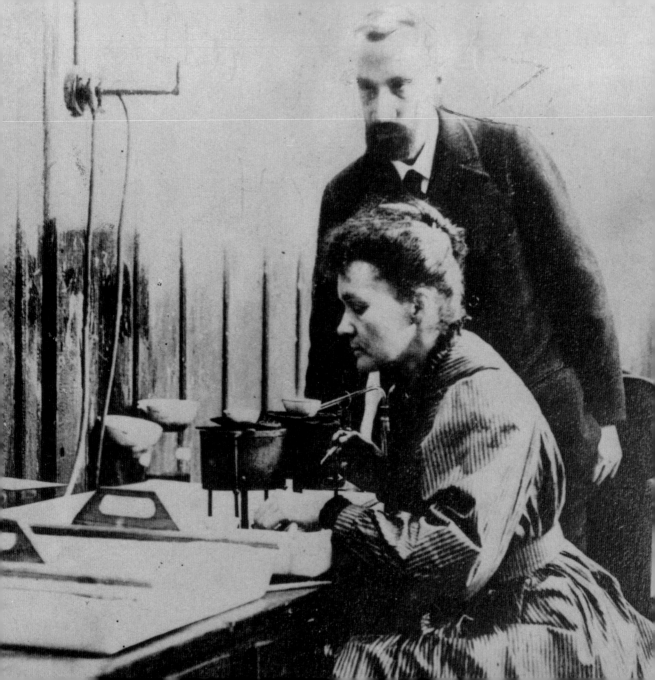

In fact, Marie and Pierre discovered two new elements in 1898. They called the first "polonium," in honor of Marie's native Poland. They called the second "radium," because of its rays.

The Curies worked tirelessly on their experiments.

A VERY FAMOUS WOMAN

In 1903, Marie and Pierre shared the Nobel Prize in physics. Pierre Curie died in 1906. In 1911, Marie won the Nobel Prize in **chemistry**. She died on July 4, 1934.

The world remembers Marie Curie not only as one of the greatest scientists, but also as one of the most famous women who ever lived.

President Warren G. Harding escorts Marie Curie from the White House during her 1921 visit to the United States.

IMPORTANT DATES TO REMEMBER

1867	Maria Sklodowska is born in Poland
1891	Maria moves to Paris, France, to enter the Sorbonne and changes her name to Marie
1895	Marie marries Pierre Curie
1898	Marie and Pierre experiment with uranium and discover polonium and radium
1903	The Curies share the Nobel Prize for physics with another scientist
1906	Pierre dies
1911	Marie wins the Nobel Prize in chemistry
1934	Marie Curie dies

GLOSSARY

chemistry (KEM uh stree) — the science of the elements and their differences

element (EL uh munt) — the most basic part of anything, which, in chemistry, cannot be broken down or divided into something else

experiments (ek SPARE uh muntz) — tests of something

laboratory (LAB uh ruh TOR ee) — a place where a scientist does experiments; sometimes called a "lab"

physics (FIZ icks) — the science of energy and physical matter

radium (RAYD ee um) — an element discovered by Marie and Pierre Curie

scholarship (SKAHL ur SHIP) — money awarded to pay for some or all of a student's education

scientists (SI unt ists) — people who study nature and how it works

uranium (yu RAY nee um) — an element

INDEX

Further Reading

Rau, Donna Meachen. *Marie Curie.* Compass Point Books. 2000.
Schaefer, Lola M. *Marie Curie.* Pebble Books. 2004.

Websites to Visit

http://www.aip.org/history/curie/
http://www.ideafinder.com/history/inventors/curie.htm

About the Author

Don McLeese is an associate professor of journalism at the University of Iowa. He has won many awards for his journalism, and his work has appeared in numerous newspapers and magazines. He has written many books for young readers. He lives with his wife and two daughters in West Des Moines, Iowa.

AR-4.1